Energy and
Natural Resources

Researched and written by Reference Services, Central Office of Information.

© Crown copyright 1992
Applications for reproduction should be made to HMSO.
First published 1992
ISBN 0 11 701700 0

HMSO publications are available from:

HMSO Publications Centre
(Mail, fax and telephone orders only)
PO Box 276, London SW8 5DT
Telephone orders 071-873 9090
General enquiries 071-873 0011
(queuing system in operation for both numbers)
Fax orders 071-873 8200

HMSO Bookshops
49 High Holborn, London WC1V 6HB
(counter service only)
071-873 0011 Fax 071-873 8200
258 Broad Street, Birmingham B1 2HE
021-643 3740 Fax 021-643 6510
Southey House, 33 Wine Street, Bristol BS1 2BQ
0272 264306 Fax 0272 294515
9-21 Princess Street, Manchester M60 8AS
061-834 7201 Fax 061-833 0634
16 Arthur Street, Belfast BT1 4GD
0232 238451 Fax 0232 235401
71 Lothian Road, Edinburgh EH3 9AZ
031-228 4181 Fax 031-229 2734

HMSO's Accredited Agents
(see Yellow Pages)

and through good booksellers

Photo Credits

Numbers refer to the pages in the illustration section (1–8): Ironbridge Gorge Museum Trust p. 1 (top); Mr Christopher Sugg and Sugg Lighting Limited p. 2 (bottom); British Gas p. 2 (top), p. 3 (bottom); BRECSU p. 2 (bottom); Subsea Offshore Limited p. 3 (top left); Shell UK Limited p. 3 (top right); British Coal p. 4 (top); COI p. 4 (bottom); Scottish Nuclear Limited p. 5 (top); ETSU p. 5 (bottom), p. 6 (top and bottom); Wave Energy Group, Queen's University of Belfast p. 7 (top); ECC International p. 7 (bottom left); Thames Water plc p. 7 (bottom right); North West Water p. 8 (top); Welsh Water—Dŵr Cymru p. 8 (bottom).

The front cover photo of sand and gravel working is by courtesy of BACMI.

Contents

Introduction

Energy and non-fuel minerals make an important contribution to the British economy. The approximate value of minerals produced in 1990 was £16,803 million (representing just over 4 per cent of gross domestic product—GDP), of which crude oil accounted for 48 per cent, coal 23 per cent and natural gas 15 per cent.

All minerals in Great Britain are mainly privately owned, with the exception of gold, silver, oil and natural gas (which are owned by the Crown), and coal and some minerals associated with coal. In Northern Ireland gold and silver are owned by the Crown, while rights to exploit petroleum and other minerals, except common substances, including aggregates, are vested in the Department of Economic Development. On the United Kingdom Continental Shelf the right to exploit all minerals except coal is vested in the Crown. The exclusive right to extract coal, or license others to do so, both on land in Great Britain and under the sea, is vested in the British Coal Corporation.

Normally, ownership of minerals belongs to the owner of the land surface, but in some areas, particularly those with a long history of mining, these rights have become separated. Mining and quarrying, apart from deep coalmining, are usually carried out by privately owned companies.

Energy Management

Resources

Britain has the largest energy resources of any country in the European Community and is a major world producer of oil, natural gas and coal—called primary sources. The other main primary sources are nuclear power and some water power; secondary sources (derived from primary sources) are electricity, coke and smokeless fuels, and petroleum products. In 1991 Britain was a small net importer of energy, amounting to 13.8 million tonnes of oil equivalent. In financial terms, however, the higher value of its exports meant that it was a net exporter of energy, to the value of £104 million. There are large reserves of coal, which is expected to continue to supply a significant proportion of the country's energy needs. Nuclear power provided about 21 per cent of electricity supplied by the British electricity companies in 1991.

Private sector companies carry out offshore oil and gas production and oil refining, while a publicly owned body is at present responsible for most coal production. The electricity supply industry in Great Britain, apart from nuclear power, has been privatised. The privatisation of the electricity supply industry in Northern Ireland is in train.

Energy Policy

In 1992 the functions of the former Department of Energy were transferred to the Department of Trade and Industry, with the exception of energy efficiency, which was transferred to the Department of the Environment. The President of the Board of Trade and the Secretary of State for the Environment are thus responsible for energy matters in Great Britain, except for electricity in Scotland, which is under the Secretary of State for Scotland. The Secretary of State for Northern Ireland is responsible for all energy matters there.

Energy policy is designed to ensure the secure, adequate and economic provision of energy to meet Britain's requirements. The Government encourages the exploitation of Britain's diverse energy sources. It seeks to ensure that all economic forms of energy are produced, supplied and used as efficiently as possible, having regard also to the international application and environmental implications of the technologies involved. Central government spending on energy is planned to decline by over 50 per cent between 1991–92 and 1994–95, with an increasing share of expenditure directed at non-nuclear items and at energy efficiency.

The Government stresses the importance of the continued profitable development of Britain's oil and gas resources, the development of a competitive coal industry, the safe and economic development of nuclear power, and the most cost-effective use of energy through the adoption of energy efficiency measures. It also funds an extensive research and development programme into renewable sources of energy.

Privatisation
Privatisation has already had an impact in the energy field, with the transfer of British Gas, Britoil, Enterprise Oil, and the non-nuclear electricity supply industry in Britain to the private sector. The Government wishes to privatise the coal industry during the present Parliament. It considers that privatised industries improve

their competitiveness and efficiency, free of government pressures, and attract new investment to provide cheaper and cleaner energy.

The Competition and Service (Utilities) Act 1992 aims to give customers of privatised utilities fair treatment and strengthens the powers of regulators. Customers are to be compensated when standards are not met and greater competition introduced into the gas industry.

International Commitments

Britain is actively engaged in international collaboration on energy questions, notably through its membership of the European Community and of the International Energy Agency (IEA; a body with 23 member countries attached to the Organisation for Economic Co-operation and Development). In 1990 the European Community introduced the THERMIE scheme for the promotion of energy technology, including support for demonstration projects in the hydrocarbons sector.

European Energy Charter

In 1991 Britain (along with member states of the Community and EFTA, eastern European countries, the republics of the former Soviet Union, the United States, Japan, Australia and Canada) signed the European Energy Charter. Associated legally binding agreements are under negotiation. The main objectives are:

—an open competitive market for trade in energy, including a framework for investment promotion and protection;

—co-operation in the energy field, through, for example, co-ordination of energy policies and mutual exchange of technical data; and

—promotion of energy efficiency and environmental protection, including the use of new and renewable sources of energy.

Energy Use and the World Environment
Britain stresses that energy efficiency (see p. 7), with its role in combating the threat of climate change, is the cornerstone of any sustainable energy policy, both in Europe and throughout the world. Global warming is caused by the gases in the atmosphere which absorb radiated heat—greenhouse gases. Human activity builds up more and more greenhouse gases, such as carbon dioxide (CO_2) and nitrous oxide (N_2O). Britain is taking steps, with other countries, to reverse the upward trend in CO_2 emissions. It believes that the problem must be tackled through an international framework, otherwise rapid changes in climate could have serious effects on crops, cause drought and flooding, damage natural systems, spread disease and halt economic development.

Consumption

During 1980–91, when Britain's GDP increased by 25 per cent, final energy consumption on a 'heat supplied' basis increased by only 8.4 per cent. Energy consumption by final users in 1991 amounted to 61,302 million therms[1] on a 'heat supplied' basis, of which transport consumed 31.1 per cent, industrial users 26 per cent, domestic users 29 per cent, and commerce, agriculture and public services 13 per cent.

[1] 1 therm = 105,506 kilojoules

Table 1: Inland Energy Consumption (in terms of primary sources)

million tonnes of oil equivalent

	1981	1986	1989	1990	1991
Oil	65.2	66.2	69.5	71.3	71.1
Coal	69.6	66.8	63.6	63.8	63.3
Natural gas	42.4	49.2	47.4	49.0	52.8
Nuclear energy	8.0	12.5	15.2	14.2	15.2
Hydro-electric power	1.4	1.4	1.4	1.6	1.4
Net imports of electricity	–	3.1	3.0	2.9	3.9
Total	186.6	197.2	200.2	202.7	207.7

Source: Department of Trade and Industry.
Note: Differences between totals and the sums of their component parts are due to rounding.

Table 2: Energy Consumption by Final Users (heat supplied basis)

million therms

	1986	1989	1990	1991
Industry	16,208[1]	15,759	15,390	15,266
Transport	16,258	18,834	19,306	19,044
Domestic	17,348	16,073	16,191	17,876
Public administration	3,544	3,049	3,045	3,246
Agriculture	565	502	504	514
Miscellaneous	3,898	4,114	4,177	4,504

Source: Department of Trade and Industry.

[1]Includes fuel used at power stations owned by industry, and excludes electricity generated at those power stations. For later years, includes electricity generated but excludes fuel used in generation.

Energy Efficiency

The Energy Efficiency Office (EEO), established in 1983 and part of the Department of the Environment, provides a wide range of services and programmes designed to encourage cost-effective energy efficiency improvements. The EEO promotes its programmes through its restructured and strengthened network of regional energy efficiency officers. Since 1983, EEO programmes have cost some £190 million and have led to annual savings now worth over £500 million a year. The EEO's budget has been increased to £59 million in 1992–93.

Consumers in Britain spent £49,000 million (including taxes) on energy in 1990—9 per cent of GDP. Of this amount, the EEO estimates that about 20 per cent could have been saved if consumers had invested in cost-effective energy efficiency measures.

The Government stresses that improved energy efficiency not only saves valuable energy resources, but also has a significant role to play in achieving the Government's environmental objectives. It also helps to reduce acid rain pollution, which is caused mainly by the sulphur dioxide (SO_2) and oxides of nitrogen (NOx) formed when coal and oil are burnt, mostly in power stations.

Public Sector Campaign

All major government departments and English health authorities have been set a target to reduce energy consumption by 15 per cent over five years. Energy efficiency in local authorities and schools is also being promoted.

Best Practice

The EEO's main technical information transfer and research and development programme, Best Practice, aims to advance and spread good practice in energy efficiency by providing energy users, building professionals and those responsible for industrial production with a wide range of advice and information. Work under the Best Practice programme is managed by the Energy Technology Support Unit (ETSU; for industry) and the Building Research Energy Conservation Support Unit (BRECSU; for buildings) and consists of four parts:

1 *Energy Consumption Guides* give data on energy consumption in specific processes, operations, plant and building types. Organisations may use these guides to compare their energy usage with that of others either in their sector or occupying similar buildings.

2 *Good Practice Guides and Case Studies* give information on what improvements in energy efficiency are being achieved by the most efficient users in each sector, and how this is being done.

3 *New Practice* projects monitor the first commercial applications of new energy efficiency measures which do not yet have wide market acceptance, and provide independent reports on the operation of those measures.

4 *Future Practice* provides support for club projects in pre-competitive research and development to develop new energy efficiency measures.

The aim of the Best Practice programme is to stimulate additional savings of £700 million a year at 1992 prices by the year 2000.

The part of the Best Practice programme which deals with research and development is designed to stimulate further energy efficiency technologies. It is managed by ETSU and BRECSU.

Combined Heat and Power

The EEO promotes the wider use of Combined Heat and Power (CHP) technology, primarily through its Best Practice programme. CHP plant produces usable heat as well as electricity, making it significantly more efficient than conventional energy options. This can lead to substantial energy cost savings and also makes CHP an environmentally friendly technology. CHP is operated on over 600 sites in Britain. It has a total installed capacity of some 2,000 megawatts (MW).[2] This accounts for about 3 per cent of electricity generated.

Energy Management Assistance Scheme

This scheme, introduced in 1992, aims to help companies with 500 employees or fewer to invest in energy efficiency. The budget is £13 million over three years. Assistance is limited to costs incurred by consultants hired by the client. Only one application may be made by an organisation during each financial year. There is an upper limit on grants of £25,000 (excluding value added tax) for organisations employing between 300 and 500 people. A similar scheme has been introduced in Northern Ireland.

Home Energy Efficiency Scheme

The EEO's Home Energy Efficiency Scheme provides grants for draughtproofing, insulation of lofts, tanks and pipes, and energy efficiency advice to low-income households in both public and private sector housing. Its main aim is to boost the adoption of these basic measures. Householders are eligible if they receive income support, housing benefit, family credit or community charge support. Separate arrangements to provide assistance for energy efficiency measures to low income households apply in Northern Ireland.

Energy Efficiency Campaigns

In 1991 the EEO and the Department of the Environment launched a three-year, £10-million, advertising and publicity campaign, called *Helping the Earth Begins at Home*, to improve understanding of the greenhouse effect and the impact of domestic energy use on the environment. The EEO has also launched a promotional campaign, *Making a Corporate Commitment*, aimed at directors. It is designed to motivate industrial, commercial and public sector organisations to make a corporate commitment to responsible energy management.

Energy Efficiency Demonstration Programme

The Government's Energy Efficiency Demonstration Programme funds over 70 schemes to improve energy efficiency and reduce CO_2 emissions from council houses in England. Some £50 million is available in 1992–93.

Energy Saving Trust

In 1992 the Department of the Environment, British Gas, and the regional electricity companies in England and Wales agreed to establish an Energy Saving Trust to develop programmes to promote the efficient use of energy. Of three pilot schemes, one will promote sales of high efficiency condensing boilers.

[2] 1 MW = 1,000 kilowatts (kW).

Energy Labelling

Britain has been working with its European Community partners on the development of effective legislative measures on appliance labelling. A framework directive for mandatory energy labelling of domestic appliances has been agreed. Until the first labels appear, the EEO and regional electricity companies have developed an interim voluntary scheme to put energy efficiency labels on appliances, starting with refrigerators and freezers, sold in the companies' 1,100 showrooms throughout Great Britain.

A standard assessment procedure for comparing home energy labels produced by different schemes, designed by the Building Research Establishment, has been launched—to be used in the National Energy Foundation and MVM Starpoint schemes. A home energy labelling certificate tells a householder how energy efficient his or her house is and generally contains advice about cost-effective measures which can be taken to improve a property's energy efficiency and cut fuel bills.

Oil and Gas

Britain's energy position is strengthened by substantial oil and gas reserves offshore in the United Kingdom Continental Shelf (UKCS). The trend in offshore oil and gas developments is towards the exploitation of smaller reservoirs, and the advances in science and technology (for example, seismic acquisition technology, reservoir characterisation and subsea production systems) have made this a more economic proposition.

Full-scale exploration for oil and natural gas in the UKCS began in 1964. The first commercial gas discovery (the West Sole field) was made in 1965 and production started two years later. The first oilfield in the UKCS was discovered in 1969 and oil production started in 1975 in the Argyll field.

Fifteen significant offshore discoveries were announced in 1991: six of gas, five of oil, three of gas condensate, and one of oil and gas. The Government has granted exploration and production licences as a result of 12 offshore licensing rounds since 1964. The Government announced two separate offshore licensing rounds in April 1990: the twelfth round and the thirteenth (frontier) round. In May 1991, 74 twelfth round awards were announced, covering 107 blocks. The thirteenth (frontier) round awards were also announced in May 1991; six awards were made covering 66 blocks. The thirteenth round was aimed at promoting exploration of deep water areas north and west of Scotland. By the end of 1991, 4,846 wells had been or were being drilled in the UKCS: 2,198 development wells, 1,660 exploration wells and 988 appraisal wells.

In the fourteenth round, announced in March 1992, licensed acreage on offer will include remaining acreage in the main mature areas of the northern, central and southern North Sea; more speculative acreage on the margins of the main mature areas; and true frontier acreage where any finds will take a long time to prove.

Offshore Supplies

The Offshore Supplies Office (OSO) of the Department of Trade and Industry aims to promote fair commercial opportunity in all oil and gas markets, to support development of the latest technologies and to stimulate British exports.

In 1991 the total value of orders reported by operators for oil and gas development work on the UKCS was £6,079 million, close to the 1990 figure, at £6,186 million the highest ever. The British share in 1991 was £4,734 million (78 per cent). The total value of orders placed in 1991 for goods and services in support of onshore activity was £38.5 million. British supply companies are also estimated to be winning a share of the available market for offshore work beyond the North Sea, worth about £2,000 million a year. Just under one-third of all offshore work won by British industry is for exports.

In 1991 OSO assisted British companies to obtain more support than any other Community member state for the hydrocarbon sector of the THERMIE scheme (see p 4), winning about 30 per cent of the funds distributed. It also added 47 research and development projects to its offshore technology programme, on which it spent some £3.4 million.

At the end of 1991 the latest in a series of initiatives to promote collaboration between British and Norwegian supplies companies took place. It is aimed at small- and medium-sized companies.

Research

Advice on the direction and content of the OSO's research and development in offshore technology is provided by the Offshore Energy Technology Board. The Petroleum Science and Technology Institute, set up in Edinburgh in 1989, is funded by 35 oil companies and the OSO. Its remit is to support oil-related research in British universities. The Offshore Technology Park in Aberdeen comprises several projects and is part-funded by Scottish Enterprise.

Table 3: The Highest-producing Oil and Gasfields in 1991 (with cumulative totals since 1975)

Oilfields	(1,000 tonnes)	Gasfields	(million cubic metres)
Alwyn North	3,995 (15,310)	Alwyn North	3,145 (11,859)
Beryl	4,596 (65,985)	Audrey	2,097 (7,035)
Brent	8,518 (180,404)	Hewett and Della	2,612 (101,805)
Forties	8,172 (282,389)	Indefatigable	3,899 (109,741)
Fulmar	4,992 (58,678)	Leman	7,451 (261,157)
Magnus	6,352 (51,428)	Ravenspurn	4,078 (5,808)
Ninian	4,247 (124,971)	Victor	1,845 (11,374)
Statfjord (UK)	4,612 (46,372)	Vulcan	1,717 (5,742)

Source: *Development of the Oil and Gas Resources of the United Kingdom 1992.*
Department of Trade and Industry.

Economic and Industrial Aspects

In 1991 UKCS oil and gas production accounted for about 1.5 per cent of Britain's gross national product at factor cost. Total revenue from the sale of oil and gas produced from the UKCS in 1991 is estimated to have been £8,000 million and £2,800 million respectively. Taxes and royalty receipts attributable to UKCS oil and gas are estimated to have been £1,000 million in 1991–92— £1,500 million lower than in 1990–91, because of lower oil prices and higher investment.

Expenditure on offshore and onshore development amounted to some £5,100 million in 1991. This was about 21 per cent of British industrial investment and 5 per cent of gross domestic fixed capital formation. Total investment between 1965 and 1991 came to about £46,000 million (£79,000 million at 1991 prices). Some 33,200 people were employed offshore in September 1991.

Britain's production of oil and gas in 1991 corresponded to about 42 per cent and 22 per cent of total primary fuel consumption respectively. Oil production, at 91.3 million tonnes, exceeded consumption (82.8 million tonnes, including imported products), and there was a substantial export and import trade in crude oil (see Table 4, p. 19).

Offshore Safety

Safety in such an inhospitable environment as the North Sea is seen as of paramount importance. In November 1990, the Cullen report (see p. 67) into the destruction by explosion and fire of the Piper Alpha fixed oil production platform in July 1988 resulted in 106 recommendations for a new regulatory system of offshore safety.

The Offshore Safety Act 1992 assists in enabling the major recommendations to be implemented. It clears the way for the progressive replacement of existing prescriptive offshore safety legislation by new regulations made under the Health and Safety at Work etc. Act 1974. It also raises the maximum penalties for offences which show a failure to manage health and safety adequately and to comply with an improvement or prohibition notice.

The Act will also allow the recommendations to be implemented by regulations rather than primary legislation. The Act completes the statutory transfer of offshore safety responsibilities to the Health and Safety Executive.

Offshore Environmental Protection

The United Kingdom Offshore Operators' Association has issued a statement of guiding principles to further environmental protection. They include:

—the adoption of procedures and practices to protect the environment;

—the protection of the environment when handling materials, products and waste;

—the assessment and minimisation of spills and emissions; and

—co-operation with the Government and European authorities to safeguard the environment.

Mature fields process more than four times as much water as oil. The Government stresses the need for water produced in offshore operations to be treated to meet strict environmental requirements before discharge. The offshore industry is encouraged to take the initiative in trying to anticipate events which could have consequences detrimental to the environment.

Oil

The oil industry in Britain dates back to 1850 when Dr James Young, a Glasgow chemist, succeeded in obtaining lamp oil and lubricants from natural mineral oil occurring in the Derbyshire coalfields. The Scottish shale deposits, yielding similar products, were worked between 1858 and 1962.

Britain also helped develop the vast oil resources of the Middle East, with the formation in 1909 of the Anglo-Persian Oil Company, now British Petroleum (BP), to exploit the concession of a Briton, William Knox D'Arcy. From 1901 another Briton, Weetman Pearson (later Lord Cowdray), with his Mexican Eagle Oil Company, played a major part in developing Mexico's oil resources. Thereafter BP, the Anglo-Dutch company Shell, and other British companies were pioneers in the development of mineral oil industries in Indonesia, Iraq, Nigeria, Venezuela and other countries and, more recently, in Alaska. British companies continue to provide essential services under consultancy or collaborative arrangements, while also carrying out exploration in various parts of the world.

Before the 1970s Britain was almost wholly dependent for its oil supplies on imports, the only indigenous supplies coming from a small number of land-based oilfields. However, the first notable offshore discovery of oil in the UKCS was made in 1969 and the first oil was brought ashore in 1975. Output of crude oil in Britain in 1991 averaged about 1.87 million barrels (about 256,000 tonnes) a day, making Britain the world's ninth largest producer.

North Sea Fields

There were 45 offshore fields producing crude oil at the end of 1991, and 14 new offshore development projects were approved during the year.

The fields with the largest cumulative production totals are Forties and Brent. Ninian, Piper, Beryl, Fulmar and Magnus are other high-producing fields. Production from most large fields is controlled from production platforms of either steel or concrete which have been built to withstand severe weather, including gusts of wind of up to 260 km/h (160 mph) and waves of 30 m (100 ft). The Petroleum Act 1987 lays down measures to be taken in connection with the abandonment of offshore installations and pipelines.

Output is likely to increase until the mid-1990s, and Britain should remain self-sufficient in oil well into the 1990s and a significant producer into the twenty-first century. The Government's oil policy encourages exploration, development and investment, with the objective of maximising economic oil production for the foreseeable future.

Reserves

Remaining recoverable reserves of UKCS oil in the proven plus probable categories amount to 1,230 million tonnes, while the total remaining potential of the UKCS could be as high as 7,180 million tonnes.

Structure of the Oil Industry

About 250 companies, including many large oil firms, operate in Britain or engage in work in the UKCS. Exploration and development of the UKCS are carried out by the private sector. The Government receives royalties from UKCS oil.

The two leading British oil companies are BP and Shell Transport and Trading, which has a 40 per cent interest in the Royal Dutch/Shell Group of Companies. BP and Shell are the two largest industrial companies in Britain in terms of turnover. BP's group turnover for 1991 was £32,613 million; the Royal Dutch/Shell Group of Companies' sales revenue from oil, gas and coal was £66,756 million. BP Exploration's worldwide development programme includes exploration in frontier regions, such as the People's Republic of China, Vietnam and West Africa.

Table 4: Oil Statistics

million tonnes

	1981	1986	1989	1990	1991
Oil production[a]					
land	0.2	0.5	0.7	1.8	3.7
offshore	89.3	126.5	91.1	89.8	87.6
Refinery output	72.0	74.1	81.4	82.3	85.5
Deliveries of petroleum products for inland consumption	66.3	69.2	73.0	73.9	74.5
Exports (including re-exports) crude petroleum, natural gas liquids (NGLs) and feedstocks	52.2	87.4	51.7	57.0	55.1
refined petroleum products	12.3	15.3	16.7	16.9	19.4
Imports crude petroleum, NGLs and feedstocks	36.9	41.2	49.5	52.7	57.1
refined petroleum products	9.4	11.8	9.5	11.0	10.1

Source: Department of Trade and Industry.

[a] Crude oil plus condensates and petroleum gases derived at onshore treatment plants.

Land-based Fields

Onshore production of crude oil is much less significant than off-shore production. In 1991, however, it increased by 110 per cent to 3.7 million tonnes, 85 per cent of which came from Britain's largest onshore field at Wytch Farm (Dorset), which started production in 1979. In addition to minor production from various mining licensees, other onshore fields include Humbly Grove and Stockbridge (Hampshire), Palmers Wood (Surrey), Nettleham and Welton (Lincolnshire) and Wareham (Dorset). Small, independent companies play an increasingly prominent role in onshore exploration. At the end of 1991, 194 landward petroleum licences were in force, covering an area of 29,647 sq km (11,447 sq miles).

Refineries

At the beginning of 1992 the distillation capacity of Britain's 11 major oil refineries stood at 90 million tonnes a year. Excess crude distillation capacity has largely been eliminated, while existing refineries have been adapted to the changing pattern of demand by the construction of upgrading facilities (for example, 'catalytic crackers'), which are leading to a higher output of lighter products, mainly petrol, at the expense of fuel oil.

Consumption and Trade

Deliveries of petroleum products for inland consumption (excluding refinery consumption) in 1991 totalled over 74 million tonnes, including:

—24 million tonnes of motor spirit;

—8 million tonnes of kerosene;

—19.3 million tonnes of gas and diesel oil (including derv fuel used in road vehicles); and

—12.1 million tonnes of fuel oil.

Virtually all exports of crude oil went to Britain's partners in the European Community and the IEA, the largest markets being The Netherlands, France, Germany, Canada and the United States. Though self-sufficient, Britain continues to import other crude oils, to enable the full range of petroleum products to be made efficiently and economically.

Oil Pipelines

Oil pipelines brought ashore about 74 per cent of offshore oil in 1991. Some 1,934 km (1,202 miles) of major submarine pipeline brings oil ashore from the North Sea oilfields. Major crude oil onshore pipelines in operation from harbours, land terminals or offshore moorings to refineries include those connecting Grangemouth to Finnart, Cruden Bay to Grangemouth and Purbeck to Southampton. Onshore pipelines also carry refined products to major marketing areas: for example, a 423-km (263-mile) pipeline runs from Milford Haven to the Midlands and Manchester, while similar pipelines run from Fawley to Wolverhampton and from Lidsey to north London. Chemical pipelines include one from Mossmorran to Grangemouth and another (405 km—252 miles) from Grangemouth to Stanlow. Newly built natural gas pipelines, not operated by British Gas plc, run from Horndean to Barking and from Theddlethorpe to Killingholme.

Gas

The growth of the gas industry in Britain followed the experiments of William Murdock who, in 1792, used gas obtained from coal to light a room in his house in Redruth (Cornwall). Britain, with large coal reserves, was a pioneer in the commercial development of gas; its first public supply was installed in 1807 with the lighting of Pall Mall in London.

For many years gas was produced from coal, but during the 1960s growing imports of oil brought about production of town gas from oil-based feedstocks. Following the first commercial natural gas discovery in the UKCS in 1965 and the start of offshore gas production in 1967, supplies of offshore natural gas grew rapidly and by 1977 natural gas had replaced town gas in the public supply system in Great Britain. Some £12,000 million has been spent on developing natural gas resources in the UKCS and over 840,000 million cubic metres have been produced.

Structure

The gas industry in Great Britain, in state ownership since 1949, was privatised in 1986. British Gas plc supplies gas to consumers in accordance with its authorisation as a public gas supplier under the Gas Act 1986. It is currently the only public gas supplier. It has, however, an obligation to act as a common carrier for other companies. There are currently eight independent companies which supply gas in competition with British Gas, using the company's transport network.

The regulatory regime for the private gas sector was established by the Gas Act 1986 and places responsibility on the Office of Gas Supply (Ofgas) for ensuring that British Gas is operating within the terms of its authorisation as a public gas supplier. The Act also established the Gas Consumers' Council, independent of both British Gas and Ofgas, and responsible for investigating consumer complaints. The Competition and Service (Utilities) Act 1992 increased Ofgas's powers and provided for the compensation of customers when standards are not met and for more competition in the supply of gas services.

British Gas has about 2.2 million private and institutional shareholders. In 1991 the turnover of British Gas and its subsidiary companies amounted to £10,485 million, of which gas supply in Britain accounted for £8,423 million. Current cost operating profit was £1,673 million. British Gas has just over 74,000 employees in Britain.

Production

In 1991 indigenous production of natural gas amounted to 55,242 million cubic metres. This includes 3,444 million cubic metres of gas used for drilling, production and pumping operations on North Sea production platforms and at terminals. Total sales of UKCS gas amounted to 52,000 million cubic metres—11.9 per cent higher than in 1990. In addition, 7,000 million cubic metres of gas were imported from Norway. British production of gas accounts for some 20 per cent of total primary fuel consumption in Britain. Natural gas from the seven largest of the 35 gasfields—Leman, Indefatigable, Ravenspurn North, Hewett and Della, Vulcan, Audrey and Victor—accounted for about one-third of the total gas produced in the UKCS. In addition to supplies from gasfields, associated gas delivered to land via the Far North Liquids and Associated Gas System (FLAGS) and from Alwyn North made further significant contributions. Gas from the South Morecambe field in the Irish Sea and from the twin North Sean and South Sean fields is used to augment supplies to meet peak demand in winter.

Reserves

Remaining recoverable gas reserves are estimated at between 540,000 million and 1.8 million million cubic metres. If possible gas from existing discoveries and potential future discoveries is added; total reserves are estimated to be in the range of 1.74 million million to 4.17 million million cubic metres. Indigenous offshore natural gas reserves are likely to meet most of the British demand well into the next century.

Transmission and Storage

The British Gas national and regional high-pressure pipeline system of some 17,600 km (11,100 miles) transports natural gas around Great Britain. It is supplied from four North Sea shore terminals, and from a terminal in Barrow-in-Furness (Cumbria). The high-pressure transmission system is inspected regularly.

Various methods of storage of natural gas to meet peak load conditions are used, including salt cavities and storage facilities for liquefied natural gas. British Gas has also developed the partially depleted Rough field as a major gas store. This, the first such use of an offshore field, involves the injection into the Rough reservoir in summer of gas drawn from the national transmission system for recovery at high rates during periods of peak winter demand.

Consumption

Sales of gas by the supply industry in Britain totalled 20,220 million therms in 1991. About 31 per cent of all gas sold by British Gas to its 18 million consumers is for industrial and commercial purposes, the remainder being for domestic use. Gas is used extensively in industries requiring the control of temperatures to a fine degree of accuracy, such as the pottery industry, and in certain processes for making iron and steel products. In 1991, 5,284 million therms of gas were sold to industry in Britain, and 3,457 million therms to commercial and other non-domestic users. An increasingly large part of domestic demand is for gas for central heating. In 1991, 11,479 million therms were sold to domestic users.

Competition in Gas Marketing

The gas market in Britain is being progressively liberalised. Following a review by the Office of Fair Trading of competition in the industrial and commercial gas market in Britain, British Gas gave undertakings in 1992 designed to increase competition. It agreed to reduce its share of the industrial and commercial contract gas market from 95 per cent to 40 per cent in 1995 and to set up a separate transportation and storage unit. Further, the Government signalled its intention in 1992 to reduce British Gas's statutory monopoly threshold in the supply market, thus enabling smaller industrial and commercial users to benefit from competition.

Research

British Gas has a worldwide reputation for gas technology, with a research programme costing £90 million in 1991. It is involved in joint research with overseas gas companies. Its technology transfer group is assisting utilities in over 20 countries in transmission, distribution and other areas. British Gas is today exploring for and producing gas and oil in some 20 countries.

Coal

Coalmining in Great Britain can be traced back to Roman times. Mining activity was in progress in the thirteenth century. Output in 1700 was about 3 million tonnes; in 1800 about 15 million tonnes; and in 1850 about 63 million tonnes. It played a crucial part in the industrial revolution of the eighteenth and nineteenth centuries, and in its peak year, 1913, the industry produced 292 million tonnes of coal, exported 74.2 million tonnes and employed over a million workers.

In 1947 the coalmines passed into public ownership, and the National Coal Board (now the British Coal Corporation) was set up. Production remained at about 220 million tonnes a year into the late 1950s. Coal accounted for 90 per cent of British primary energy consumption in 1950, but growing competition from other fuels led to a decline in its market.

The Government has introduced legislation to privatise the coal industry. It intends to repeal the Coal Mines Regulation Act 1908, which relates to hours of work and is no longer considered relevant to the modern coal industry. It has reduced the debt under which the industry was operating and eliminated accumulated liabilities incurred by British Coal. Through restructuring grants it also assists British Coal's expenditure on redundancy and early retirement, transfers, retraining and British Coal Enterprise (see below).

British Coal Corporation

British Coal has, with limited exceptions, exclusive rights over the extraction of coal in Great Britain. It is empowered to license private operators to work mines with an employee limit of 150 and opencast sites with a production limit of 250,000 tonnes so that underground and opencast deposits too small for British Coal to work can be usefully exploited. It also has powers to work other minerals, where discoveries are made in the course of searching for, or working, coal; and to engage in certain petrochemicals activities beneficial to the future of the coal industry.

Production

Rationalisation of the industry in recent years has entailed British Coal improving its productivity and reducing its costs to ensure effective competition. Increases in productivity (reaching some 6 tonnes in one manshift) have been accompanied by a programme of pit closures. In 1991–92 total output of 91.1 million tonnes comprised 71 million tonnes of deep-mined coal, 16.7 million tonnes from opencast mines and 3.4 million tonnes from licensed mines. At the end of March 1992 there were 50 British Coal collieries in operation, compared with 850 in 1955. At the same date its workforce was 58,000, of whom 44,000 were miners, compared with 695,000 miners in 1955. British Coal Opencast also had 58 sites in operation at the end of March 1992. Since 1984 British Coal, through its job creation activity, British Coal Enterprise, has helped create job opportunities for 76,500 people in areas where mining was previously the main source of employment.

Licensed Mines

At the end of 1991–92 there were 142 privately owned mines with licences to work coal underground in Britain. These produced just over 1 million tonnes of coal and employed some 1,650 people. There were also 77 privately owned opencast sites in operation in Britain. Output totalled 1,667,000 tonnes in England and Wales and 635,000 tonnes in Scotland.

Development

Britain's coal industry is the largest hard-coal industry in western Europe, and one of the world's most technologically advanced. British Coal has a substantial investment programme, which amounted to £286 million in 1991–92. Technical progress has been concentrated on equipment capable of obtaining higher output from fewer faces. By mid-1992 79 per cent of all coal faces were equipped with heavy duty supports available across the full range of seam thicknesses. Production at the new mining complex at Selby in North Yorkshire (one of the world's most advanced deep mines) is planned to produce up to 10 million tonnes a year. The development of a new mine at Asfordby within the Vale of Belvoir (Leicestershire) is in progress.

Significant reserves of lignite (brown coal) have been discovered in Northern Ireland in the clay basins around Lough Neagh and at Ballymoney. Companies under government licence are prospecting to determine their extent, possibly over 1,000 million tonnes.

Consumption

In 1991–92 inland consumption of coal was 105 million tonnes, of which:

—76.7 per cent was by power stations;

—9.5 per cent by coke ovens; and

—5 per cent by domestic users.

With a substantial proportion of coal being used by power stations for electricity generation, British Coal sales of coal to them totalled 73 million tonnes in 1991–92. Exports of coal in 1991–92 were 1.4 million tonnes, while imports amounted to 20 million tonnes.

Research

Over £500 million has been spent by the public sector in Britain on coal utilisation research and development since the early 1980s. Some £1,000 million has been spent if all coal research and development work is included.

The Government's and British Coal's principal research objective is to make the burning of coal more environmentally acceptable. It aims to reduce emissions of SO_2, NOx, CO_2 and other gases associated with the greenhouse effect. The British Coal topping cycle development programme is designed to improve the efficiency of combined cycle power generation to 45 per cent. It offers a 20 per cent reduction in CO_2 emissions from coal-fired power stations. Further studies into combined cycle power plant worked by coal gasification have been possible through the British Coal gasification development programme. A number of projects aimed at reducing NOx emissions in pulverised coal combustion have government support, some in collaboration with the IEA.

In five new projects, worth nearly £20 million and designed to promote the clean and efficient use of coal, the Government is collaborating with British Coal, British industry, other countries (including the European Community) and the IEA. The projects involve underground gasification, the relation between greenhouse gases and fossil fuel use, and NOx.

The coal liquefaction plant at Point of Ayr (Clwyd), opened in 1990 at a cost of £40 million and converts 2.5 tonnes of coal a day into petrol, diesel and other transport fuels. The Government will also be considering the work carried out by its coal task force, which reviewed clean coal technologies and technologies aimed at maximising economically recoverable coal from Great Britain's coal reserves.

Electricity

The first public supply of electricity in Britain was at Godalming (Surrey) in 1881 and in 1882 the first power station to generate electricity for public supply began operating at Holborn Viaduct in London. Electricity generation was developed by local authorities and private sector companies, but a measure of public control was always a feature of the industry. In the 1930s a mainly regional 132kV (kilovolt) transmission system was constructed and connected to form a national grid. In the 1950s and 1960s a more extensive national transmission system was built. It operated at 275 kV and 400 kV, and was known as the super-grid. As a result, the size and efficiency of power stations rose and their number fell. Electricity from the supply system is available to all premises in Britain except for some very remote households.

In 1990-91 certain parts of the electricity supply industry were restructured and sold.

Restructuring after Privatisation

The privatised electricity supply industry in England and Wales consists of three main generating companies, the National Grid Company (NGC) and 12 regional electricity companies (RECs). The two main non-nuclear generators, National Power and PowerGen, the publicly owned nuclear generator, Nuclear Electric plc, and other generators and importers sell electricity to suppliers through a market known as the pool. The NGC operates the transmission system—the bulk transfer of electricity across the national grid—and owns the pumped storage stations at Dinorwig and Ffestiniog (Gwynedd). It is owned by the RECs through a holding company. Distribution and supply of electricity are the business of the RECs. Distribution involves transfer of electricity from the national grid and its delivery, across local systems, to consumers. Supply is the sale of electricity to customers. Each REC is authorised to supply any premises within its area. Other companies may obtain a second-tier licence to supply, although initially competition is limited to premises with a maximum consumption of 1 MW.

The Government retains approximately 40 per cent of the issued ordinary share capital of each of National Power and PowerGen, and will not sell, or otherwise dispose of, this holding before 1 April 1993.

Restructuring in Scotland created three companies. Two vertically integrated companies, ScottishPower plc and Scottish Hydro-Electric plc, generate, transmit, distribute and supply electricity. They are also contracted to buy all the output from Scottish Nuclear Ltd, a government-owned company which operates the nuclear power stations at Hunterston (Strathclyde) and Torness (Lothian), and have contracts to share the output from each other's generation capacity. Opportunities exist to export and import electricity to and from the pool (see above). The boundary separating the ScottishPower and Scottish Hydro-Electric supply areas runs from Loch Long on the Firth of Clyde to Newburgh on the Firth of Tay.

Certain service and co-ordinating functions for the industry are carried on by the Electricity Association, jointly owned by the electricity companies of Great Britain. Regulation of the industry is the responsibility of the Office of Electricity Regulation, headed by the Director General of Electricity Supply, whose duties include the promotion of competition and the protection of consumer interests.

Northern Ireland

Generation, transmission and supply of electricity in Northern Ireland have hitherto been carried out by Northern Ireland Electricity, a public corporation. Privatisation of the industry is in train: the trade sale of Northern Ireland's four power stations is complete and the flotation of the transmission and supply system (NIE plc) is due to take place late in 1992.

There are plans, subject to detailed undersea survey, to link Northern Ireland with the Great Britain gas network through the construction by British Gas of a gas pipeline to Northern Ireland and the conversion of the Ballylumford station to gas firing.

Consumption

In 1991 sales of electricity through the distribution system in Britain amounted to 277,550 gigawatt hours (GWh).[3] Domestic users took 36 per cent of the total, industry 34 per cent and commercial and other users the remainder. About 24 per cent of domestic sales is for space heating, 13 per cent for water heating and 8 per cent for cooking. Electricity is used in industry mainly for motive power, melting, heating and lighting.

Generation

National Power owns 35 operational fossil-fuelled power stations, which generate about 46 per cent of the electricity supplied to the transmission and distribution networks in England and Wales. PowerGen owns 19 fossil-fuelled power stations, which generate some 30 per cent of this electricity. The 12 nuclear stations of Nuclear Electric generate about 17 per cent.

[3] 1 GW = 1,000 MW.

In 1991–92, 40 per cent of electricity supplied in Scotland was produced by Scottish Nuclear's two stations. The power stations operated by ScottishPower and Hydro-Electric provided most of the balance. ScottishPower has 15 power stations and in 1991–92 its three coal-fired stations produced 50.2 per cent of the electricity supplied in its area, with nuclear power contributing 43.5 per cent. Hydro-Electric has 59 stations (mostly hydro, but with one major oil/gas station), and in 1991–92 they produced 61.9 per cent of the electricity supplied in its area, with nuclear power contributing 22.5 per cent. All of Scottish Nuclear's production is sold to ScottishPower and Hydro-Electric in the proportions 74.9 per cent and 25.1 per cent respectively.

Non-nuclear power stations owned by Britain's major generating companies consumed 69.2 million tonnes of oil equivalent in 1991, of which coal accounted for 70 per cent and oil 10 per cent. The declared net capacity of these stations at the end of March 1992 totalled 69,323 MW.

Independent generators are allowed to compete on equal terms with the major generators and have equal access to the grid transmission and local distribution systems.

To control acid emissions the Government expects National Power and PowerGen each to fit flue gas desulphurisation (FGD) equipment to 4 GW of their existing coal-fired power stations. Work is in progress towards fitting FGD equipment to National Power's Drax (North Yorkshire) station. For its part, ScottishPower expects to fit FGD as necessary at the Longannet station. In addition, a ten-year programme to control NOx emissions through the installation of low NOx burners at the 12 largest power stations in England and Wales, at a cost of approximately £185 million, is also in progress. The Scottish companies are expected to fit low NOx burners at the main coal stations.

Table 5: Generation by and Capacity of Power Stations owned by the Major Generating Companies in Britain

| | Electricity generated (GWh) | | | Output | |
| | | | | Per cent capacity[a] | |
	1981	1986	1991	1991	(MW)
Nuclear plant	34,043	54,005	66,329	15	10,733
Other steam plant	220,259	221,426	229,190	74	51,365
Gas turbines and oil engines	509	509	358[b]	5	3,136[b]
Pumped-storage plant	1,003	2,221	1,523	4	2,787
Natural flow hydro-electric plant	3,917	4,098	3,777	2	1,302
Total	259,731	282,258	301,176	100	69,323
Electricity supplied (net)[c]	242,106	261,160	280,649		

Source: Department of Trade and Industry.

[a] At 31 March 1992.

[b] These figures include generation by and capacity of wind power stations.

[c] Electricity generated less electricity used at power stations (both electricity used on works and that used for pumping at pumped-storage stations).

Note: Differences between totals and the sums of their component parts are due to rounding.

Combined Cycle Gas Turbines

For new stations the trend is towards the construction of combined cycle gas turbines (CCGTs). They are less costly to build than other types of station, and have shorter construction times and lower capital costs. Their use of natural gas, low in sulphur, also helps to reduce acid and CO_2 emissions. The installation of the more efficient CCGT plant should also help to stabilise CO_2 emissions from the electricity supply industry. In England and Wales, nine such stations over 50 MW have been given planning consent under the Electricity Act 1989. Britain's first independent CCGT station, in Cumbria, was opened in 1991. It has a generating capacity of 230 MW and its output will be fed into the local distribution system, representing 7 per cent of the local REC's demand.

Pumped-storage Schemes

The pumped-storage station at Dinorwig, the largest of its type in Europe, has an average generated output of 1,728 MW. Pumped-storage schemes at Cruachan and Foyers (Highland) have a total capacity of 700 MW. In pumped-storage schemes electricity generated in off-peak periods is used to pump water to high-level reservoirs from which it descends to drive turbines, rapidly providing a large supply of electricity at peak periods or to meet sudden increases in demand.

Interconnectors

The NGC, together with Electricité de France, runs a 2,000-MW cross-Channel cable link, providing the capacity for the transmission of electricity between the two countries. Transmission lines linking the Scottish and English grid systems enable cross-border trading. This interconnector is run jointly by the NGC and ScottishPower. Its capacity is planned to be increased from 850 MW to 1,600 MW by 1994–95.

Northern Ireland Electricity and ScottishPower have agreed to construct a 250-MW interconnector between Scotland and Northern Ireland, to come into operation in 1996.

Nuclear Power

In 1956, the world's first industrial-scale nuclear power station, at Calder Hall (Cumbria), began to supply electricity to the national grid. There are 14 operating commercial nuclear power stations that generate electricity in Britain: seven magnox stations (with capacities ranging from 245 to 840 MW) and seven Advanced Gas-cooled Reactor stations (AGRs; ranging from 720 MW to 1,320 MW). Construction of a pressurised water reactor (PWR) of 1,175 MW at Sizewell (Suffolk) is expected to be completed in 1994. There are also two magnox stations, Berkeley (Gloucestershire) and Hunterston A (Strathclyde), which have been shut down and are in the process of being decommissioned.

The Government recognises two main advantages to continued nuclear power generation:

1 Nuclear power increases diversity of energy supply and thus helps maintain its security;

2 Nuclear power can play a part in curbing acid rain and in combating global warming. Nuclear stations emit no SO_2, NOx and CO_2. If the electricity currently provided by nuclear were to be generated from coal, emissions of carbon would increase by 15.5 million tonnes a year.

The Government wishes to maintain the nuclear option, but only if nuclear power becomes more competitive with other energy sources. One reason for nuclear being more expensive than fossil fuels is that it is the only source of generation which bears the environmental costs of its fuel cycle. The relative costs would improve

Coalbrookdale (Shropshire) ironworks (close to supplies of low-sulphur coal), where Abraham Darby I first smelted iron with coke in 1709.

An early exercise in energy efficiency: the incandescent Christiania burner lights, introduced by William Sugg in 1874, gave the consumer better results.

Heat from a gas-fired combined heat and power unit at a leisure centre in Irvine (Strathclyde) not only provides warm water for the swimming pools, but also heats the centre.

Cavity wall insulation helps warm the home and plays a part in reducing CO_2 emissions to the atmosphere.

A remotely operated vehicle (ROV), built by Subsea of Aberdeen, tackling a wellhead fire.

The intelligent pig, an inspection vehicle developed by British Gas, uses ultrasonics and magnetic waves to check pipelines.

The Shell/Esso Eider oil production platform in the North Sea, north-east of the Shetlands.

Renewing a gas main in Aberdeen – by lining the existing cast-iron pipe with flexible polyethylene pipe.

Heavy duty coalface at Wistow colliery, one of five mines which form
the Selby (North Yorkshire) mine complex.

Drax power station (North Yorkshire), where flue gas desulphurisation equipment is being
fitted to help protect the environment.

The two nuclear power stations at Hunterston on the Ayrshire shore of the Firth of Clyde are owned and operated by Scottish Nuclear Ltd. Hunterston A magnox station (*left*) was shut down in 1990 after 25 years' service and is now being decommissioned. Hunterston B advanced gas-cooled reactor supplies over 20 per cent of Scotland's electricity.

A 300-kW capacity horizontal axis wind turbine (28m diameter) at Burgar Hill (Orkney), built by James Howden and Co. Ltd of Glasgow with support from the Department of Trade and Industry, has produced electricity for the local grid since 1983.

BP's 30-kW photovoltaic system at Marchwood (Southampton).

A house using passive solar design at Chorley (Lancashire).

Britain's first shoreline wave energy system, developed by Queen's University, Belfast, uses an air-driven turbine to convert energy from waves entering a rock gully into electricity.

Littlejohns Clay Pit, near St Austell, Cornwall.

Building Thames Water's London ring main (average width 2.5 m and depth 40 m).

North West Water's Haweswater reservoir (Cumbria; 5.5 km long), created in 1937 when the valley and village of Mardale were flooded.

Court Farm water treatment works, near Caerleon (Gwent).

A fish farm, Cynrig hatchery, near Llanfrynach (Powys), owned by the National Rivers Authority.

if environmental costs of fossil fuel were taken into account on a comparable basis.

The Government intends to carry out a full-scale review of nuclear power in 1994, but before then the Government and the industry will take several initiatives, which include:

—improving the efficiency of nuclear stations, extending the lives of existing nuclear stations if it is safe and economic to do so, and completing the PWR at Sizewell B to time and to cost;

—speeding up investigations into a potential repository for radioactive waste;

—carrying out a full-scale review of civil nuclear research and development; and

—commissioning further research into the medical aspects of radiation.

Fossil Fuel Levy
In England and Wales the Government has introduced a 'fossil fuel levy', which is currently set at 11 per cent, on electricity sales. Most of the revenue raised is used to pay a premium to nuclear generators, as the cost of producing energy from nuclear sources is greater than that of producing it from fossil fuel sources. The premium is, however, set to be phased out by 1998, by which time it is hoped that nuclear power generation will be economically competitive.

British Nuclear Fuels
British Nuclear Fuels plc (BNFL) provides services covering the whole nuclear fuel cycle. All of its shares are held by the Government. The company, with headquarters at Risley (Cheshire), conducts operations at four further sites:

—Springfields (Lancashire), where fuel is manufactured;

—Capenhurst (Cheshire), where uranium is enriched to provide fuel for nuclear reactors;

—Sellafield (Cumbria), where Calder Hall is located and where spent fuel is reprocessed; and

—Chapelcross magnox power station (Dumfries and Galloway).

A substantial investment programme is in progress, mainly at Sellafield. BNFL's major project is the thermal oxide reprocessing plant (THORP), construction of which has now been completed at a cost of some £2,800 million, including its share of associated facilities. THORP will reprocess spent fuel from British and overseas oxide reactors and is expected to start operations early in 1993. At the same time, BNFL will bring into operation the latest of its waste management and effluent treatment facilities. The enhanced actinide removal plant (EARP) will use a revolutionary ultra-filtration process to provide further treatment facilities for low-level radioactive waste.

Nuclear Research

The nuclear research and development funded by the Department of Trade and Industry is carried out by the United Kingdom Atomic Energy Authority's (UKAEA) nine semi-autonomous businesses, which operate as AEA Technology. The work is carried out at six sites: Harwell and Culham (Oxfordshire), Risley and Winfrith (Dorset), Windscale (Cumbria) and Dounreay (Highland). In addition, safety research is carried out by AEA Safety and Reliability at Culcheth (Cheshire).

Co-operation on nuclear energy between Britain and other countries takes place within a framework of intergovernmental agreements and membership of bodies such as the International Atomic Energy Agency and the Nuclear Energy Agency, as well as through direct links on research between AEA Technology and equivalent organisations overseas.

Britain takes part in the co-operative research programmes of the European Atomic Energy Community (Euratom). A major component of this programme is the Joint European Torus (JET) project at Culham, which started operating in 1983. It has successfully carried out an experiment which, it is claimed, demonstrates the scientific feasibility of thermo-nuclear fusion. The JET device (a Tokamak) is reported to have produced an energy release equivalent to 1 MW for two seconds.

Under an agreement with its French and German counterparts, AEA Technology is carrying out research and development work for the European fast reactor collaboration. The detailed design phase of this collaboration, sponsored by the utilities in Britain, France and Germany, is due to be completed in 1993.

Nuclear Safety
Britain has a rigorous system of nuclear safety regulation, enforced by the Health and Safety Executive's Nuclear Installations Inspectorate, which ensures that high standards of safety are incorporated into the design, construction, operation, maintenance, decommissioning of all nuclear plant, and eventual disposal of resulting wastes. While the safety of such plant in Britain is the ultimate responsibility of the nuclear operator, the Inspectorate has extensive powers. An operator must satisfy it before a licence is granted. Operators must protect their workers and the public by complying with the Health and Safety at Work etc. Act 1974, as well as with the conditions of their nuclear site licences under the Nuclear Installations Act 1965. The Inspectorate has the power to shut down a plant if it is believed to be unsafe and may also require

improvements to an installation if it thinks the appropriate safety standards are not being met.

Discharges have to be kept within the limits and conditions set by authorisations granted under the Radioactive Substances Act 1960. In England and Wales separate authorisations are required from the Secretaries of State for the Environment and for Wales, and from the Minister of Agriculture, Fisheries and Food, and in Scotland from the Secretary of State for Scotland. Within maximum dose limits, operators of nuclear facilities are required to keep discharges as low as reasonably achievable and failure to do so makes them liable to prosecution. Compliance with the legislation is overseen by Her Majesty's Inspectorate of Pollution in England and Wales, and by Her Majesty's Industrial Pollution Inspectorate in Scotland.

On nuclear safety, Britain has a number of bilateral agreements and arrangements with, for example, France and the United States, covering the exchange of information relating to all matters affecting nuclear safety. International conventions have been established on the early notification of a nuclear accident with possible transboundary effects, and on the mutual provision of assistance in the event of a nuclear accident or radiological emergency.

Emergency Plans

The precautions taken in the design and construction of nuclear installations in Britain, and the high safety standards in their operation and maintenance, reduce the chance of accidents which might affect the public to an extremely low level. However, all operators are required, as a condition of their site licences, to prepare emergency plans, including those for dealing with an accidental release of radioactivity, which are regularly tested in exercises under the supervision of the Nuclear Installations Inspectorate.

Research on Electricity
Research and development are a matter for the individual companies, but some research is carried out jointly. National Power and PowerGen maintain a joint environmental programme. Technological research on generation and main transmission is undertaken primarily by the generating companies and by the NGC. The Electricity Association has also undertaken research into improving the performance of distribution systems.

Renewable Sources of Energy

The Department of Trade and Industry supports research, development and demonstration in the renewable energy technologies. It aims to exploit alternative sources of energy which have the potential to be economically viable and environmentally acceptable. It also encourages industry to develop both internal and export markets. Its current programme includes some 350 projects with a financial commitment of £87 million. Work is at present concentrated on the most promising technologies.

A total of 77 contracts, valued at £9.6 million and aimed at encouraging the commercialisation of renewable energy in Britain, formed part of the government research, development and demonstration programme in 1990–91. Of the contracts (which included two strategic studies and two general studies), 26 were for wind power, 20 for biofuels, nine for solar power, seven for tidal power, seven for wave power, two for geothermal power and two for hydro power. First established in 1974, the programme has received total government funding of £180 million. Expenditure in 1991–92 was some £24 million.

The Government is aiming at a figure of 1,000 MW of electricity generation capacity from renewable energy by the year 2000. The 1990 and 1991 Orders under the non-fossil fuel obligation in England and Wales (see p. 37) allowed for 197 renewable energy projects, with a declared net capacity of 559 MW.

Strategy Review

The Government is reviewing its renewable energy strategy. As part of that process, a ministerial advisory group has been formed to provide an independent comment on the overall review. The group's members are drawn from the renewables industry, business, management and the academic sector.

Wind Power

Wind power remains one of the most promising technologies. Wind turbines extract energy from the wind using aerofoil section blades which change lift forces into mechanical power. This mechanical power is transformed to electrical power by a gearbox and generator set. Both horizontal and vertical axis wind turbine generators are being built. The former, usually with two or three blades, has its axis of rotation parallel with the wind; the latter has its axis at right angles both to the earth's surface and to the direction of the wind, and has the advantage of responding to wind from any direction. The Government's research and development programme into wind power has cost more than £40 million over ten years. Expenditure is running at about £6 million a year. The programme for 1991-92 initiated some 25 new projects and managed about 100 projects.

If wind development programmes are successful, it is thought that Britain could generate the equivalent of about 10 per cent of current electricity consumption from wind power by the year 2025.

Among the projects supported by the Department are:

—two vertical-axis wind turbines, inaugurated in 1986 and 1990 at Carmarthen Bay (Dyfed);

—a 300-kW turbine also at Carmarthen Bay;

—a 3-MW, 60-m (200-ft) turbine, in collaboration with Scottish Hydro-Electric, on Orkney, inaugurated in 1987;

—a 1-MW, 55-m (180-ft) diameter turbine at Richborough (Kent), inaugurated in 1990; and

—two 300-kW turbines at the National Wind Turbine Centre (East Kilbride), opened in 1991.

Plans for experimental wind farms are progressing. The Government has agreed with National Wind Power to pursue collaborative projects at Cold Northcott (Durham) and Llangwyryfan (Powys), which are scheduled for completion during 1993.

Tidal Power

Tidal power is one of the most promising of the renewable technologies for large-scale electricity generation. Its exceptionally high tidal range makes the Severn estuary one of the best potential sites in the world. The Government has funded, with the Severn Tidal Power Group and the electricity supply industry, a £4.2 million study into the viability of a Severn tidal barrage (16 km—10 miles), of which a general report has been published. The Government has contributed about £900,000 towards further environmental, regional and financing studies.

Power would be transmitted by 400-kV cables from the barrage's 216 turbine generators to substations on both sides of the estuary. The average annual output of electricity is estimated at some 17 TWh[4]—7 per cent of present energy consumption in England and Wales, equivalent to a saving of 8 million tonnes of coal a year.

The Government has contributed some £5 million to three phases of studies, and £1.2 million towards a 15-month extension of the third phase, on an energy barrage on the Mersey estuary. The barrage (1.9 km—1.2 miles) would contain 28 turbines, each rated at 25 MW. Its energy output would be some 1,310 GWh.

[4]Terawatt hours. 1 TW = 1,000 GW.

Solar Power

The Government continues support for a solar programme and has invested some £14 million in it. Passive solar design is considered the best way to utilise solar energy in Britain and has already proved cost-effective in both domestic and non-domestic buildings, using their form and fabric to admit, store and distribute solar energy for heating and improving daylight. It is estimated that the adoption of passive solar measures on a wide scale could save Britain as much as £100 million on fuel bills by the year 2025 and more than four times that amount by the end of the next century. Use of solar power could also lead to the reduction of CO_2 emissions by 2 million tonnes a year by 2025. The Best Practice programme of the EEO (see p. 8) encourages this technology.

Recent advances in photovoltaics—in which treated glass plates convert sunlight directly into electricity—have suggested that photovoltaic materials incorporated into the cladding and roofing of buildings could provide competitive electricity generation. The Government is supporting a two-year assessment of photovoltaics, costing £250,000.

Biofuels

Biofuels offer possibly the largest contribution from the renewable energy resources in the medium term. The main work of the government programme is on the combustion of wastes, anaerobic digestion (particularly as applied to the production and use of landfill gas) and energy forestry. The following are the main biofuel resources and their possibilities:

—Landfill gas is a methane-rich biogas formed from the decomposition of organic waste material in landfill. The gas can be used directly to fuel kilns or boilers. It can also be used in engines or turbines to generate electricity.

Table 6: Total Use of Renewable Sources

thousand tonnes of oil equivalent

	1989	1990	1991
Solar			
passive[a]	0.1	0.1	0.1
active	8.5	8.5	8.5
Wind (onshore)	9.7	9.8	9.8
Hydro			
small scale[a]	27.6	27.9	29.8
large scale[b]	1.415.0	1,552.5	1,382.6
Biofuels			
landfill gas[c]	70.6	74.5	97.5
wood combustion[d]	163.0	163.0	163.0
straw combustion[e]	67.1	67.1	67.1
refuse combustion[f]	176.3	144.2	147.6
Other	90.6	102.6	106.2
Geothermal aquifers	0.5	0.4	0.6
Total	2,029.0	2,150.6	2,012.8

Source: *Digest of United Kingdom Energy Statistics 1992.*
[a] Approximate estimate.
[b] Excluding pumped storage stations.
[c] Data based on comprehensive survey.
[d] Approximate estimate based on the survey in 1989.
[e] Approximate estimate based on information in 1990.
[f] Sewage sludge digestion, farm waste digestion, and other combustion.

—Straw can be burnt in high temperature boilers designed to operate heating, hot water and hot air systems by the efficient and controlled combustion of solid fuels and biomass.

—Waste from domestic, industrial and commercial sources can be a valuable source of energy for space heating or industrial processes. Waste derived fuel—partially processed waste—can be burnt in a number of ways.

—Energy forestry—to produce wood for heating—emphasises short rotation, involving single-stem trees and coppicing (raising a crop from shoots produced from the cut stump of the previous crop) techniques.

—Other biofuels include farm gas, produced from animal slurry, and other forms of anaerobic digestion, using, for example, municipal solid waste.

Britain is the largest user of landfill gas as an energy source in the European Community, and is second only to the United States in its exploitation. At present 68 landfill projects are in operation, under construction or proposed. By burning methane they help to remove a potent greenhouse gas.

Britain's largest project to produce electricity from landfill gas, opened in 1991 in Bedfordshire, uses gas given off by buried municipal rubbish to generate 4 MW.

Wave Energy

Britain's first shoreline wave energy system was inaugurated in 1991 on the island of Islay, one of the outer islands off the west coast of Scotland. The small-scale gulley device was constructed from 1985 by the Queen's University of Belfast, which is carrying out a complementary study to assess the potential for shoreline devices in Britain. The system is rated at 75 kW and is connected to the local grid. A report on the review of wave energy is expected during 1992.

Small-scale Hydro

Small-scale hydro power was the original energy source for the industrial revolution in the eighteenth and nineteenth centuries. The turbines that drive the electricity generators are powered by the direct action of water, either from a reservoir or from the run of the river.

Generation schemes with outputs below 5 MW are classified as small scale: either turbines or waterwheels used for domestic or farm purposes, or for sales to the local REC. The Government urges organisations interested in small-scale hydro electricity generation to take advantage of government assistance in funding feasibility studies. Some £70,000 has so far been committed to 27 studies, with outputs of up to 5 MW. The first Order of the non-fossil fuel obligation allows for 26 small-scale hydro schemes, with a net capacity of 11.6 MW.

Geothermal Energy
Under its geothermal hot dry rock programme, during 1976-91, the Government investigated, through work carried out in Cornwall by the Camborne School of Mines, the economic possibilities of extracting heat from rocks at a depth of 2 to 6 km (1.25 to 4 miles). It has concluded that further funding should go largely towards participating in a joint programme with France, Germany and the European Community, which could resolve some of the technical uncertainties.

Non-Fuel Minerals

Although much of Britain's requirement for industrial raw materials is met by imports, non-fuel minerals produced in Britain make an important contribution to the economy. Britain is currently self-sufficient in construction aggregates. Output of non-fuel minerals in 1990 totalled 318 million tonnes, valued at £1,993 million. The total number of employees in the extractive industry was some 47,700 in 1990.

Exploration
Exploration for, and exploitation of, indigenous mineral resources to meet the needs of industry are encouraged by the Government. The British Geological Survey is carrying out a long-term programme for the Department of Trade and Industry aimed at identifying areas with the potential for the economic extraction of minerals. Exploration for gold, for example, continues, especially in Scotland, Northern Ireland and south-west England.

Production
In terms of value, production of limestone and dolomite was estimated at £594 million in 1990, sand and gravel £543 million, clays £270 million, igneous rock £241 million, sandstone £78 million, potash £63 million, chalk £48 million, silica sands £43 million, salt £37 million, gypsum and anhydrite £22 million, fuller's earth £15 million, fluorspar £13 million and tin £11 million. In 1990 the production of metals in non-ferrous ores totalled 12,500 tonnes, mainly tin and zinc from Cornwall. The two remaining Cornish tin

mines, one of the very few sources of tin in the European Community, produced over 3,500 tonnes in 1990, satisfying about half of Britain's demand. Wheal Jane mine was closed early in 1991. South Crofty mine continues in production. Small amounts of copper and silver were produced in association with tin and zinc, and some lead and zinc with barytes and fluorspar. A little gold came from a mine in north Wales.

Table 7: Production of Some of the Main Non-Fuel Minerals

			million tonnes
	1980	1985	1990
Sand and gravel	104.5	107.7	124.0
Silica sand	5.7	4.2	4.1
Igneous rock	34.7	38.5	57.4
Limestone and dolomite	88.8	95.5	123.3
Chalk [a]	14.0	12.0	13.1
Sandstone	12.6	13.2	18.0
Gypsum	3.4	3.1	3.5
Salt, including salt in brine	7.2	7.1	6.4
Common clay and shale	19.8[a]	18.9[a]	16.2
China clay	2.8	2.9	3.0
Ball clay	0.8	0.6	0.8
Fireclay	1.2	0.8[a]	0.9[a]
Iron ore	0.9	0.3	0.06
Potash	0.5	0.6	0.8
Fluorspar	0.2	0.2	0.1
Fuller's earth	0.2	0.2	0.2

Source: British Geological Survey, *United Kingdom Minerals Yearbook 1991.*
[a] Great Britain only.

Water

Public water supply has a long history. Hull was empowered by royal charter in 1447 to supply water, and Plymouth's first Water Act dates back to 1585. In 1609–13 Hugh Myddelton cut the New River—62 km (39 miles) long—which brought water from springs in Hertfordshire to a reservoir in Clerkenwell and gave London an additional supply of clean water. Water was first piped to the city of Edinburgh in 1621. In 1698 the engineer William Yarnold sought an Act of Parliament 'for better supplying the Town of Newcastle upon Tyne with fresh water', thus forming one of the first water companies (see below).

Under the Public Health Act 1848, which laid the basis for a series of statutes dealing with public health, a number of statutory water undertakings were established to provide water to the expanding urban population. The water supply system developed rapidly, although in piecemeal fashion with some overlapping. The achievements of later nineteenth-century engineers were considerable. Britain has acquired an international reputation for its water technology over the last century or more, after the nationwide development of water and sanitation systems.

Rainfall, River Flow and Groundwater

Average annual rainfall in Great Britain is about 1,100 mm (43 inches), but varies from a maximum of over 4,000 mm (157 inches) in the highest parts of Scotland, the Lake District and north Wales to about 500 mm (20 inches) in parts of south-east England.

Rainfall is normally well distributed throughout the year, but, on average, March to June are the driest months and September to January the wettest. Evaporation over much of Britain averages 470 mm (18.5 inches) a year, but the seasonal contrasts are large; over three-quarters of the annual total is normally concentrated in the summer half-year (April to September). As a consequence, the residual rainfall (rainfall minus evaporation) to sustain river flows and replenish reservoirs and aquifers is also highly seasonal; minimum rates of river flow generally occur in the late summer or early autumn. Average annual run-off for Great Britain as a whole is about 630 mm (24.8 inches), but large areas in the south and east record, on average, less than 150 mm (5.9 inches).

The recent past has been marked by unusual weather patterns and notable spatial and temporal variations in rainfall. The year 1990, for example, was the wettest on record for Scotland, while some districts of the English lowlands experienced their second driest year this century. By early 1992, drought conditions in parts of eastern England had persisted for well over three years. There is no close, modern parallel to the magnitude and duration of the corresponding rainfall deficiency; river flows and groundwater levels were exceptionally depressed in the late autumn of both 1990 and 1991. The drought generally achieved its greatest intensity in those lowland regions which, on average, receive the least rainfall.

In Britain there are some 6,000 rain-gauges, some 1,200 river-flow measurement stations and over 3,000 wells and boreholes from which data are regularly collected and processed. The Meteorological Office is the authority concerned with rainfall information. Responsibility for the national archives of river flow data and groundwater level data rests with the Institute of Hydrology and the British Geological Survey respectively.

Supplies

Britain's water supplies are obtained partly from surface sources such as mountain lakes, streams impounded in upland gathering grounds and lowland river intakes, and partly from underground sources by means of wells, springs, adits and boreholes. About 99 per cent of the population in Great Britain and 97 per cent in Northern Ireland are connected to the public water supply system. Water put into the public supply system in England and Wales amounted to about 17,370 megalitres (Ml) a day in 1990–91 and average daily domestic consumption per head was 140 litres.

Table 7: Water Supplied by Country

megalitres a day

	1981	1985	1988	1990–91
England and Wales:				
Metered	4,591	4,541	4,623	4,832
Unmetered	11,223	12,036	12,365	12,536
Scotland:				
Metered	674	658	629	656
Unmetered	1,588	1,540	1,576	1,645
Northern Ireland:				
Metered	161	169	151	143
Unmetered	502	509	509	538

Source: *Digest of Environmental Protection and Water Statistics*, No. 14, 1991.
Note: Unmetered water includes leakages from mains and water used in firefighting.

In England and Wales up to a third of water for public supply is obtained from groundwater sources. Reservoirs impounding river flows are built to ensure the availability of supplies when natural flows are low during dry periods.

Some 35,250 Ml a day were abstracted in England and Wales in 1990, of which public water supplies accounted for 18,336 Ml a day. The electricity generating companies and other industry took some 16,400 Ml a day. Agriculture took just over 500 Ml a day.

Water consumption has steadily increased as population and living standards have risen, although with some temporary falls in consumption, as in the droughts of 1976, 1984 and 1989, mainly affecting England and Wales. Since 1980-81 the rise in demand for water has been slower, reflecting the falling demand for industrial water.

England and Wales

The Water Act 1989 privatised the utility functions of the ten former water authorities in England and Wales. It provided for the Secretaries of State for the Environment and for Wales, the Director General of Water Services and the National Rivers Authority (NRA) to be the principal regulators of the industry. The Minister of Agriculture, Fisheries and Food and the Secretary of State for Wales are responsible for policy relating to land drainage, flood protection, sea defence, and the protection and development of fisheries. The Drinking Water Inspectorate was set up to regulate drinking water quality.

Water Companies

The ten water service companies are the principal operating subsidiaries of the ten water holding companies. They have statutory responsibilities for water supply, sewerage and sewage treatment, and for ensuring adequate supplies. The supply-only companies, of which there were in 1989 already 29 in the private sector, supply water to about a quarter of the population.

The Water Industry Act 1991 allows the water companies to determine their own methods of charging. At present most charges are based on the former rateable value system, although customers may choose to pay to have a water meter installed. In general, companies require new properties to have metered supplies. An alternative to the system based on rateable values, however, must be found by the year 2000. Wide-scale water metering is one of the choices being considered.

A system of economic regulation and guaranteed standards of service is overseen by the Director General of Water Services. His/her main tasks are to ensure that the companies carry out, and finance, their functions properly and secure reasonable returns on their capital; and to promote competition, where appropriate, between existing undertakers, and with new entrants.

Water Quality

The Water Supply (Water Quality) Regulations 1989 define wholesomeness and incorporate the requirements of the European Community's drinking water directive. They impose physical, chemical and microbiological standards for water intended for domestic and food production purposes. The task of the Drinking Water Inspectorate is to ensure that drinking water is wholesome and that companies comply with the Regulations. Its first annual report (see Further Reading, p. 64) found that out of 3.3 million tests carried out on drinking water during 1990, 99 per cent came within the legal limits.

National Rivers Authority

The NRA, the environmental regulator, is a non-departmental public body with statutory duties and powers in relation to water resources, pollution control, flood defence, fisheries, recreation, conservation and navigation in England and Wales. The water environment for which it has responsibility includes all rivers, lakes, reservoirs, estuaries, coastal waters and water stored naturally underground. The NRA's consent is needed for the abstraction of water and for discharges to water.

Development Projects

The water industry in England and Wales is committed to a ten-year investment programme costing over £28,000 million at 1989–90 prices. The Government considers that adequate profitability is essential to help finance investment: for example, in replacing or renovating old distribution systems.

Thames Water is constructing an 80-km (50-mile) distribution system to meet the growing demand for water in London. This is due to be completed in 1996. North West Water has a major 25-year programme of investment to clean up the polluted rivers of the Mersey Basin.

Water is an increasingly scarce resource. The industry, through contingency planning and publicity campaigns, aims to encourage the wise use of water, especially when supplies run low because of prolonged warm, dry weather. A national review of water consumption and conservation, prompted by the drought in south, south-east, and eastern England which began in 1988, has been put in hand by the Government.

The NRA has published a survey of the prospects for public water supplies to the year 2011 in England and Wales. It is investigating the strategic development of water resources, including major new transfer schemes, and is reviewing the possibilities of a national grid and desalination.

Scotland

In Scotland responsibility for public water supply, sewerage and sewage disposal rests with the nine regional and three islands councils (the 'water authorities'). In addition, the Central Scotland Water Development Board is responsible for developing new sources of supply to provide water in bulk to the regional councils in an area of 25,900 sq km (10,000 sq miles) in central Scotland. Capital expenditure by local authorities on water and sewerage in Scotland will amount to over £700 million in the three years to 1994–95. The Secretary of State for Scotland is responsible for promoting conservation of water resources and provision by water authorities and water development boards of adequate water supplies. He has a duty to promote the cleanliness of rivers and other inland waters, and the tidal waters of Scotland. River purification authorities have a statutory responsibility for water pollution control. Compliance is monitored by the local authorities and the Scottish Office Environment Department.

The water authorities' statutory responsibility for maintaining and monitoring the quality of public water supplies is contained in the Water Scotland Act 1980. The standard of wholesomeness is set out in the Water Supply (Water Quality) (Scotland) Regulations 1990, which reflect the standard set for supplies in England and Wales. Duties are also placed on the islands and district councils and on the Secretary of State to ensure that water authorities carry out all their responsibilities in relation to complying with the quality requirements.

Water is charged for according to type of consumer: domestic consumers pay community water charges (from April 1993, council water charges); non-domestic consumers pay by means of non-domestic water rates, or through metered charges. Charges and rates are decided by each authority.

Scotland has a relative abundance of unpolluted water from upland sources. An average of 2,300 Ml a day was supplied in Scotland in 1990–91.

Northern Ireland

The Department of the Environment for Northern Ireland is responsible for public water supply and sewerage throughout Northern Ireland. It is also responsible for the conservation and cleanliness of water resources and, with the Department of Agriculture for Northern Ireland, may prepare a water management programme with respect to water resources in any area. There is a domestic water charge which is contained in the regional rate, while agriculture, commerce and industry pay metered charges. There are abundant potential supplies of water for both domestic and industrial use. An average of 681 Ml of water a day was supplied in 1990–91.

Research

Several organisations and centres of expertise provide water research services to government, the NRA, water companies and the Scottish river purification boards. The Water Research Centre is a private company with a large programme of research into environmental issues, treatment processes, mains and pipeline rehabilitation, and drinking water safety. The Natural Environment Research Council (NERC) also has a considerable programme. The relevant institutes are the Institute of Hydrology, the Plymouth Marine Laboratory, the British Geological Survey Hydrogeology Unit and the Institute of Freshwater Ecology. Research carried out by these NERC institutes embraces river modelling, water quality, climate change effects on water resources, the impact of pollution on freshwater, and estuarine and marine ecology. Among its various roles the Institute of Hydrology studies the statistics of floods and droughts.

Addresses

British Coal, Hobart House, Grosvenor Place, London SW1X 7AE.

British Gas plc, Rivermill House, 152 Grosvenor Road, London SW1V 3JL.

British Geological Survey, Keyworth, Nottinghamshire NG12 5GG.

British Nuclear Fuels plc, Risley, Warrington, Cheshire WA3 6AS.

Department of the Environment, 2 Marsham Street, London SW1P 3EB.

Department of the Environment for Northern Ireland, Stormont, Belfast BT4 3SS.

Department of Trade and Industry, Ashdown House, 123 Victoria Street, London SW1E 6RB.

Electricity Association, 30 Millbank, London SW1P 4RD.

Energy Technology Support Unit, AERE Harwell, Didcot, Oxfordshire OX11 0RA.

Institute of Energy, 18 Devonshire Street, London W1N 2AU.

Institute of Hydrology, Maclean Building, Crowmarsh Gifford, Wallingford, Oxfordshire OX10 8BB.

Institute of Petroleum, 61 New Cavendish Street, London W1M 8AR.

National Grid Company plc, National Grid House, Sumner Street, London SE1 9JU.

National Power plc, Sudbury House, 15 Newgate Street, London EC1A 7AU.

National Rivers Authority, Rivers House, 30-34 Albert Embankment, London SE1 7TL.

Northern Ireland Department of Economic Development, Netherleigh, Massey Avenue, Belfast BT4 2JP.

Northern Ireland Electricity, Danesfort, 120 Malone Road, Belfast BT9 5HT.

Nuclear Electric plc, Barnett Way, Barnwood, Gloucester GL4 7RS.

Office of Electricity Regulation, Hagley House, Hagley Road, Edgbaston, Birmingham B16 8QG.

Office of Gas Supply, 105 Victoria Street, London SW1E 6QT.

Office of Water Services, Centre City Tower, 7 Hill Street, Birmingham B5 4UA.

Offshore Supplies Office, Alhambra House, 45 Waterloo Street, Glasgow G2 6AS.

PowerGen plc, 53 New Broad Street, London EC2 1JJ.

Scottish Hydro-Electric plc, 16 Rothesay Terrace, Edinburgh EH3 7SE.

Scottish Nuclear Limited, 3 Redwood Crescent, Peel Park, East Kilbride G74 5PR.

Scottish Office Development Department, St Andrew's House, Edinburgh EH1 3DD.

Scottish Office Industry Department, New St Andrew's House, Edinburgh EH1 3TA.

ScottishPower plc, Cathcart House, Spean Street, Glasgow G44 4BE.

United Kingdom Atomic Energy Authority, Harwell, Didcot, Oxfordshire OX11 0RA.

United Kingdom Nirex Limited, Curie Avenue, Harwell, Didcot, Oxfordshire OX11 0RH.

Water Companies Association, 1 Queen Anne's Gate, London SW1H 9BT.

Water Research Centre, Henley Road, Medmenham, PO Box 16, Marlow, Buckinghamshire SL7 2HD.

Water Services Association, 1 Queen Anne's Gate, London SW1H 9BT.

Further Reading

£

Attitudes to Energy Conservation in the Home:
Report on a Quantitative Study. Department of the
Environment. ISBN 0 11 752369 0.   HMSO   1991   10.00

Calder Hall and Chapelcross Nuclear Power Stations:
The Findings of NII's Assessment of BNFL's Long-
term Safety Review. Her Majesty's Nuclear
Installations Inspectorate.
ISBN 0 11 885539 5.   HMSO   1990   4.00

Clean Coal Technology and the Coal Market after
1993. Fifth Report of the House of Commons
Energy Committee, Session 1990–91.
    Vol. 1. Report, together with the Proceedings
    of the Committee.
    ISBN 0 10 299491 9.   HMSO   1991   10.85
    Vol. 2. Minutes of Evidence with Appendices.
    ISBN 0 10 299591 5.   HMSO   1991   27.00

Clean Coal Technology and the Coal Market after
1993. Government Observations on the Fifth
Report of the House of Commons Energy
Committee, Session 1990–91.
ISBN 0 10 206792 9.   HMSO   1991   3.10

Consequences of Electricity Privatisation.
Second Report from the House of Commons
Energy Committee, Session 1991–92.

Vol. 1. Report, together with the Proceedings
of the Committee.

ISBN 0 10 285292 8.   HMSO   1992   12.95

Vol. 2. Memoranda of Evidence.

ISBN 0 10 283692 2.   HMSO   1992   16.60

The Cost of Nuclear Power.
Fourth Report of the House of Commons Energy
Committee, Session 1989–90.

Vol. 1. Report, together with the Proceedings
of the Committee.

ISBN 0 10 220590 6.   HMSO   1990   7.85

Vol. 2. Minutes of Evidence with Appendices.

ISBN 0 10 293590 4.   HMSO   1990   16.55

Decommissioning of Oil and Gas Fields.
Fourth Report from the House of Commons
Energy Committee, Session 1990–91. Report with
Appendices, together with the Proceedings of the
Committee. ISBN 0 10 203391 9.   HMSO   1991   18.30

*Decommissioning of Oil and Gas Fields. Sixth
Special Report.* Government Observations on the
Fourth Report from the House of Commons
Energy Committee, Session 1990–91.

ISBN 0 10 258591 1.   HMSO   1991   3.75

The Department of Energy's Spending Plans, 1991–92. Sixth Report from the House of Commons Energy Committee, Session 1990–91. Report, together with the Proceedings of the Committee and Minutes of Evidence with Appendices. ISBN 0 10 250591 8.   HMSO   1991   9.80

The Department of Energy's Spending Plans. Seventh Special Report. Government Observations on the Sixth Report from the House of Commons Energy Committee, Session 1990-91.

ISBN 0 10 267191 5.   HMSO   1991   1.90

Drinking Water 1990—A Report by the Chief Inspector, Drinking Water Inspectorate.

ISBN 0 11 752483 2.   HMSO   1991   16.00

Energy: Looking to the Future.
Text of a lecture given by the Secretary of State for Energy, Mr John Wakeham, on 2 February 1991.

                              Department of Energy   1991

Energy and the Environment.
Thirteenth Report of the House of Lords Select Committee on the European Communities, Session 1990-91. ISBN 0 10 485391 3. HMSO   1991   23.00

Energy Efficiency in Domestic Electrical Appliances.
Energy Efficiency Series No. 13. A report on behalf of ETSU for the EEO.

ISBN 0 11 413424 3.   HMSO   1990   24.00

Energy Efficiency.
Third Report of the House of Commons Energy
Committee, Session 1989–90.
    Vol. 1. Report, together with the Proceedings
    of the Committee.
    ISBN 0 10 283791 0.   HMSO 1991 9.60
    Vol. 2. Memoranda of Evidence.
    ISBN 0 10 283591 8.   HMSO 1991 18.30
    Vol. 3. Minutes of Evidence.
    ISBN 0 10 283691 4.   HMSO 1991 18.30

Energy for the 1990s and Beyond. An Energy
Strategy for Northern Ireland.
    Department of Economic Development for
               Northern Ireland 1991

The Fast Breeder Reactor. Fifth Report of the
House of Commons Energy Committee, Session
1989–90.
    Vol. I. Report, together with the Proceedings
    of the Committee and Memoranda of Evidence.
    ISBN 0 10 296090 9.   HMSO 1990 11.10
    Vol II. Minutes of Evidence with Appendices.
    ISBN 0 10 211990 2.   HMSO 1990 13.25

Fifth Special Report. Government Observations on
the Third Report from the House of Commons Energy
Committee on the Flue Gas Desulphurisation
Programme, Session 1989–90. Report with an
Appendix, together with the Proceedings of the
Committee. ISBN 0 10 266290 8.   HMSO 1990 1.60

The Future of Opencast Coalmining in Wales.
Second Report from the House of Commons
Welsh Affairs Committee, Session 1990–91.
Vol 1. Report, together with the Proceedings of
the Committee. ISBN 0 10 284991 9.   HMSO   1991   7.85

*Government Observations on the Sixth Report from
the Committee (Session 1988–89) on the Energy
Policy Implications of the Greenhouse Effect.* Fourth
Special Report from the House of Commons
Energy Committee, Session 1988–89.
ISBN 0 10 261189 0.   HMSO   1989   3.60

*Harnessing the Wind: The Continuing Development
of Wind Energy Technology in Britain.*
                    Department of Energy   1989

*House of Commons Scrutiny of Energy Matters:
Report together with the Proceedings of the Committee.*
Fifth Report of the House of Commons Energy
Committee, Session 1991–92.
ISBN 0 10 231392 X.   HMSO   1992   3.80

Information on Nuclear Costs.
Third Report from the House of Commons
Energy Committee, Session 1991-92.
ISBN 0 10 231292 3.   HMSO   1992   6.20

Offshore Safety Management.
Seventh Report from the House of Commons
Energy Committee, Session 1990–91. Report,
together with the Proceedings of the Committee
and Minutes of Evidence with Appendices.
ISBN 0 10 234391 8.   HMSO   1991   18.90

Oil Prices.
Second Report of the House of Commons Energy
Committee, Session 1990–91. Report with
Appendices, together with the Proceedings of the
Committee. ISBN 0 10 215091 5.   HMSO   1991   6.50

Privatisation of Northern Ireland Electricity.
Department of Economic Development for
Northern Ireland. Cm 1469.
ISBN 0 10 114692 2.   HMSO   1991   3.60

Privatisation of Northern Ireland Electricity.
First Report of the House of Commons Energy
Committee, Session 1991–92. Report, together
with the Proceedings of the Committee and
Minutes of Evidence with Appendices.
ISBN 0 10 202592 4.   HMSO   1991   17.65

The Public Inquiry into the Piper Alpha Disaster.
Department of Energy.
ISBN 0 10 113102 X.   HMSO   1990   38.00

Renewable Energy.
Fourth Report from the House of Commons
Energy Committee, Session 1991–92.
    Vol. 1. Report with the Proceedings of the
    Committee. ISBN 0 10 290192 9.   HMSO   1992   10.75
    Vol. 2. Memoranda of Evidence.
    ISBN 0 10 289592 9.   HMSO   1992   22.20
    Vol. 3. Minutes of Evidence with Appendices.
    ISBN 0 10 289692 5.   HMSO   1992   23.80

Renewable Energy in
Britain.   Department of Energy   1991

Safety in Coal Mines. First Report of the House of
Commons Energy Committee, Session 1990–91.
Report, together with the Proceedings of the
Committee, Minutes of Evidence and
Appendices. ISBN 0 10 211791 8.   HMSO   1991   17.10

Safety in Coal Mines. Government Observations on
the First Report from the House of Commons Energy
Committee, Session 1990–91. Report with
Appendix together with the Proceedings of the
Committee. ISBN 0 10 240391 0.   HMSO   1991   3.10

The Severn Barrage Project: General Report.
Energy Paper No. 57. Department of Energy.
ISBN 0 11 412952 5.   HMSO   1989   13.95

The Work of the Nuclear Installations Inspectorate.
Health and Safety Executive.
ISBN 0 11 885473 9.   HMSO   1990   3.50

The 1988 Survey for Mineral Workings in England.
        Vol. 1. Report.
        ISBN 0 11 752365 8.   HMSO   1991   30.00
        Vols. 2 and 3. 1988 Figures and Tables.
        ISBNs 0 11 752366 6 and 0 11 752367 4.
                        HMSO 1991 36.00 and 34.00

Annual Reports and Statistics

British Coal Corporation. Report and Accounts.   BCC

British Gas plc.   BG

Development of the Oil and Gas Resources of the United Kingdom.
Department of Trade and Industry

Digest of Environmental Protection and Water Statistics.
Department of the Environment   HMSO

Digest of United Kingdom Energy Statistics.
Department of Trade and Industry   HMSO

Electricity Association.   EA

National Power plc.   National Power

National Rivers Authority.   NRA

Northern Ireland Electricity.   NIE

Northern Ireland Water Statistics.
Department of the Environment for Northern Ireland

Nuclear Electric plc.   Nuclear Electric

Office of Electricity Regulation.   Offer

Office of Gas Supply. Report of the Director General.   HMSO

Office of Water Services.   Ofwat

PowerGen plc.   PowerGen

Report of Energy Research, Development and Demonstration.
International Energy Agency

Scottish Hydro-Electric plc.   S H-E

Scottish Nuclear Limited.   Scottish Nuclear

ScottishPower plc.   ScottishPower

Statistical Review of World Energy.   BP

United Kingdom Atomic Energy Authority.   UKAEA

United Kingdom Minerals Yearbook.

        British Geological Survey   BGS

United Kingdom Nirex Ltd.   UK Nirex Ltd

Water Facts.   Water Services Association

Written by Reference Services,
Central Office of Information.

Printed in the UK for HMSO.
Dd 0294192   C30   8/92

Oil

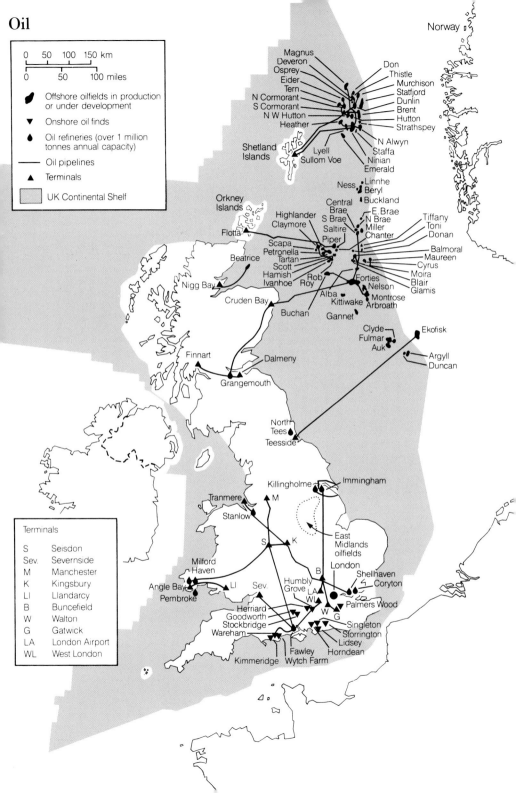

Norway

Scale:
| 0 | 50 | 100 | 150 km |
| 0 | 50 | 100 miles |

- Offshore oilfields in production or under development
- Onshore oil finds
- Oil refineries (over 1 million tonnes annual capacity)
- Oil pipelines
- Terminals
- UK Continental Shelf

Terminals

S	Seisdon
Sev.	Severnside
M	Manchester
K	Kingsbury
Ll	Llandarcy
B	Buncefield
W	Walton
G	Gatwick
LA	London Airport
WL	West London

Magnus
Deveron
Osprey
Eider
Tern
N Cormorant
S Cormorant
N W Hutton
Heather

Don
Thistle
Murchison
Statfjord
Dunlin
Brent
Hutton
Strathspey

Shetland Islands
Sullom Voe
Lyell
N Alwyn
Staffa
Ninian
Emerald

Ness
Linnhe
Beryl
Buckland

Orkney Islands

Highlander
Claymore
Central Brae
S Brae
Saltire
Piper

E. Brae
N Brae
Miller
Chanter

Tiffany
Toni
Donan

Flotta
Scapa
Petronella
Tartan
Scott
Hamish
Ivanhoe
Rob Roy

Balmoral
Maureen
Cyrus
Moira
Blair
Glamis

Beatrice

Nigg Bay

Cruden Bay

Buchan

Alba
Kittiwake
Gannet

Forties
Nelson

Montrose
Arbroath

Clyde
Fulmar
Auk

Ekofisk

Argyll
Duncan

Finnart

Dalmeny

Grangemouth

North Tees
Teesside

Killingholme
Immingham

Tranmere
Stanlow

East Midlands oilfields

Milford Haven
Angle Bay
Pembroke

Sev.

Humbly Grove

London
Shellhaven
Coryton

Palmers Wood

Herriard
Goodworth
Stockbridge
Wareham

Singleton
Storrington
Lidsey
Horndean

Kimmeridge
Fawley
Wytch Farm

Gas

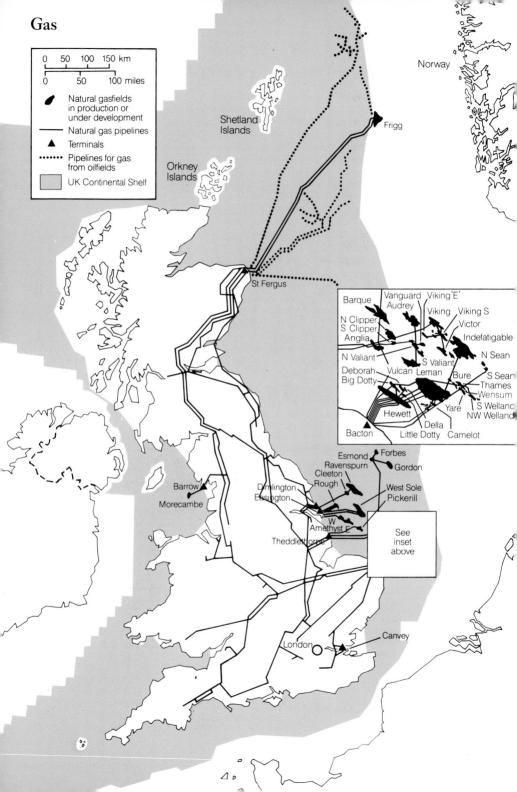

Scale
0 50 100 150 km
0 50 100 miles

- Natural gasfields in production or under development
- Natural gas pipelines
- ▲ Terminals
- ···· Pipelines for gas from oilfields
- UK Continental Shelf

Norway

Shetland Islands

Orkney Islands

Frigg

St Fergus

Barque
Vanguard   Viking 'E'
Audrey   Viking   Viking S
N Clipper   Victor
S Clipper   Indefatigable
Anglia
N Valiant   N Sean
S Valiant
Deborah   Vulcan Leman   Bure   S Sean
Big Dotty   Thames
Wensum
Yare   S Welland
Hewett   NW Welland
Bacton   Little Dotty   Camelot
Della

Esmond   Forbes
Ravenspurn   Gordon
Cleeton
Rough
Dimlington   West Sole
Easington   Pickerill

Barrow   ▲
Morecambe

See inset above

W
Amethyst E
Theddlethorpe

London ○   ▲   Canvey

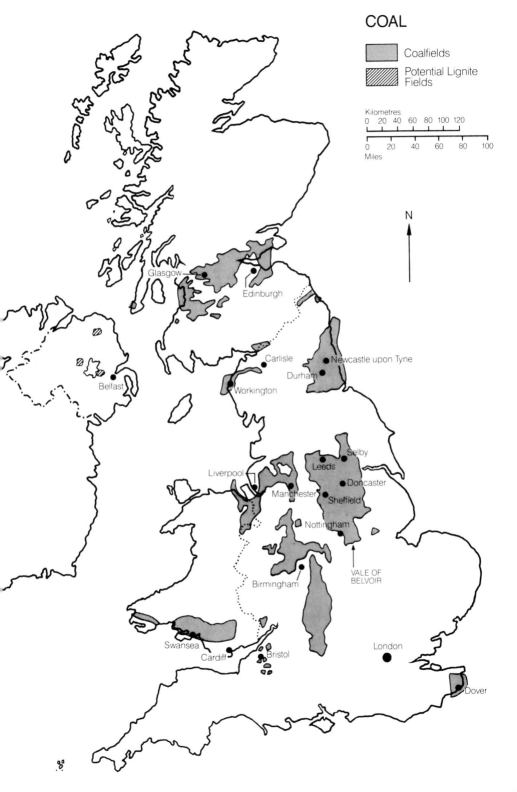

COAL

Coalfields

Potential Lignite Fields

Kilometres
0 20 40 60 80 100 120

0   20   40   60   80   100
Miles

N

Glasgow
Edinburgh
Carlisle
Newcastle upon Tyne
Durham
Workington
Belfast
Selby
Leeds
Liverpool
Doncaster
Manchester
Sheffield
Nottingham
Birmingham
VALE OF BELVOIR
Swansea
London
Cardiff
Bristol
Dover

Electricity

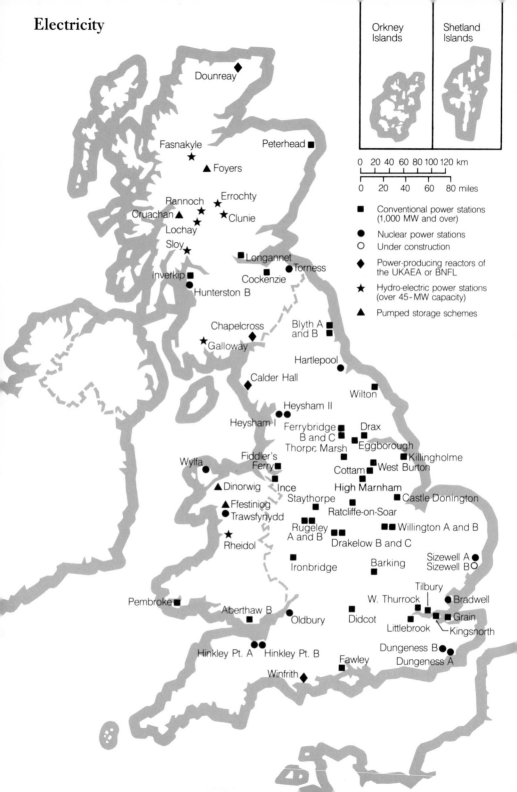

Orkney Islands

Shetland Islands

0 20 40 60 80 100 120 km

0 20 40 60 80 miles

■ Conventional power stations (1,000 MW and over)

● Nuclear power stations

○ Under construction

◆ Power-producing reactors of the UKAEA or BNFL

★ Hydro-electric power stations (over 45-MW capacity)

▲ Pumped storage schemes

Dounreay

Peterhead

Fasnakyle

Foyers

Errochty

Rannoch
Cruachan
Clunie
Lochay

Sloy

Inverkip

Longannet

Cockenzie

Torness

Hunterston B

Chapelcross

Blyth A and B

Galloway

Hartlepool

Calder Hall

Wilton

Heysham II

Heysham I

Ferrybridge B and C

Drax

Thorpe Marsh

Eggborough

Killingholme

Wylfa

Fiddler's Ferry

Cottam

West Burton

Dinorwig

Ince

High Marnham

Ffestiniog

Staythorpe

Castle Donington

Trawsfynydd

Ratcliffe-on-Soar

Rugeley A and B

Willington A and B

Rheidol

Drakelow B and C

Ironbridge

Barking

Sizewell A
Sizewell B

Tilbury

Pembroke

W. Thurrock

Bradwell

Aberthaw B

Oldbury

Didcot

Grain

Littlebrook

Kingsnorth

Hinkley Pt. A

Hinkley Pt. B

Fawley

Dungeness B
Dungeness A

Winfrith